Early Acclaim

for Surprises on the Road to Enlightenment

Thought-provoking and insightful! Paul Hoyt shares a lifetime of wisdom in a way that invites people to look within and grow. Surprises on the Road to Enlightenment is **a fabulous tool for both personal reflection and small group discussion.** What if it helps you awaken to new possibilities for soulful living?

> ~ Mindy Hart-Audlin, author of "What If It All Goes RIGHT?" and founder of The What If UP Club

Surprises on the Road to Enlightenment is a book that should be a cornerstone of any person's library who is working on becoming their best self. **The book is filled with wonderful nuggets of wisdom and life lessons** that will resonate with those on a path to personal mastery. I highly recommend this engaging and uplifting book, as well as Paul's other works.

> ~ Brett Lechtenberg – Owner, Personal Mastery Martial Arts

"Surprises," **a mesmerizing collection of profound insights**, artfully unveils Paul Hoyt's 50-year personal growth odyssey, unveiling unexpected catalysts. Amidst the challenges of sustaining awakening, Hoyt's words evoke the bittersweet allure of enlightenment. **A treasured companion for seekers of spiritual growth, this poignant book brims with wisdom and encouraging whispers of self-discovery.**

> ~ Dr. Andrea Adams-Miller, MNLP, MCHt, NFP, BFP, International Publicist, and Neuroscientist

We can never get enough wisdom, and in Surprises on the Road to Enlightenment, Paul Hoyt shares a lifetime of it! **The insights are both clear and profound,** and find myself both pondering the messages and wanting more. I'm sure some of the wisdom you already know, but I am also sure that you will be surprised and a little more enlightened once you read it. **Take a few steps towards enlightenment yourself – get this book!**

~ David M. Corbin: Consultant, Insultant, Resultant, #1 Wall Street Journal Best Selling Author, USA Today Best Selling Author, Keynote Speaker, Mentor, Inventor, Entrepreneur, and Pretty Good Guy

Paul Hoyt, the brilliant mind behind Mind Sequencing, offers a refreshing perspective on personal development in his new book, Surprises on the Road to Enlightenment. **His deep lifelong passion for understanding the nature of reality and human potential shines through his thought-provoking conversations and tireless inner work.** With a love for transformational tools that truly work, Hoyt's expertise and commitment to sharing wisdom make this book a must-read for anyone seeking a profound shift in their life's journey. **This book is the transformative guide that will undoubtedly shorten your own path to enlightenment.**

~ Tracy Hazzard – Former Inc. Columnist & CEO of Podetize

"To be with my friend Paul Hoyt is to be with one who is **fully present to life in our midst.** We both share a curiosity of finding the extraordinary in the ordinary. **Paul listens … and Grace and Joy resound.**".

~ Rev. Dr. Mark Pumphrey, Senior Pastor, Disciples of Christ (Retired)

Surprises on the Road to Enlightenment — the Wisdom of a Lifetime is **one of the most beautiful and most moving pieces of writing that I have ever had the privilege to read.** Here again, one of the greatest inspirational minds of our time has produced **a work that will lift the mind and heart of every reader** with powerful motivational appeal. Typically, if a book has one passage, one idea with the power to change a person's life, that alone justifies reading and re-reading it. This book has several such passages. **Paul has given us his precious gift of wisdom.** This book is truly an act of love!

~ Ihsaan York, CEO, House of York Films

There is a fundamental grace, or simplicity, to life. Yet we can so easily become overwhelmed with all the challenges we meet along the way. **Paul Hoyt brings us back to that grace, to that simple elegance of life, with his mindful yet powerful book.** With fundamental insights behind every chapter, Surprises on the Road to Enlightenment provides a clarity, and simplicity, to the practice of awakening. **Paul reminds us of the many ways we can find those enlightened moments woven within our everyday lives, giving us guidance to how simple shifts in our perspectives can bring us closer to our enlightened state of mind.** Enlightenment can be a daily practice, that is woven into the journey itself. Get your copy of Paul's book and bring elegance and grace into your everyday walk of life.

~ Les Jensen , Founder of New Human Living, Host of New Human Living spiritual podcast, Author of Citizen King: The New Age of Power and Forgiven Sinner: God's Last Savior

Also by Paul Hoyt

Inspirational Works

The Levels of Creation (2016)

The Practice of Awakening II: The First Light of Joy – Over 160 Awakening Lessons and Poems for You Transformational Journey (2013)

The Practice of Awakening – 150 Ways to Raise Your Consciousness Whenever You Choose (2010)

Remember – A Simple, Gentle, Powerful Pathway to Your Magnificent Potential (2005)

Business Works

Beyond Business Survival – The Key to Thriving in Business (2013)

The Capital Coaching Program (2010)

The Foundation Factor – Critical Measurements of Business Strength (2004)

SURPRISES!

ON THE ROAD TO ENLIGHTENMENT

The Wisdom of a Lifetime

Paul Hoyt

This book is dedicated to Mabel,
the sweetest little girl that I have ever known.

Table of Contents

Foreword and Acknowledgements

I've been on this journey of personal and spiritual growth for a long time – well over 50 years – and so many of the things I have learned have been surprises.

BIG surprises! **HUGE** surprises!

Humbling surprises.

And that's what this book is all about.

It is the surprises, those times when I discovered something was true that I didn't even suspect was true, the times when the universe hit me over the head with a two-by-four or kicked me in the ass, that have dramatically propelled my progress and allowed me to grow quicker.

So here they are.

My hope is that you will be delightfully surprised, too, and that your journey will take a little less time than mine. ☺

---------ooOoo---------

I've had a lot of help along the way. I am deeply grateful for the guidance from my immediate family, who top my list of supporters. Thank you Sherry, Steve, Curtis, and Alyson.

And mostly, thanks to Mabel. Just by being her precious little self, she has shown me a joy in life that I had somehow forgotten.

Suggested Practice

These insights are intentionally short – they are designed to simulate your thoughts, not to do all your thinking for you.

You may want to just blast through them, but I encourage you not to do that. Ponder the questions at the end of each Insight. Read them more than once.

Relax. Ponder. Reflect.

Listen to that Still, Small Voice.

Who knows what you will discover!

---------ooOoo---------

I encourage you to take this book with you, so you can quickly and easily read one or more messages when you have a few minutes to spare. Put it in your briefcase or purse, so you can make progress on your journey whenever you choose.

ONE

Enlightenment!

The first Surprise on the Road to Enlightenment to me was that there was such a thing as Enlightenment!

I was very surprised to hear about it. My early religious upbringing was focused on Christianity and there was no such concept in those circles. My church preached of forgiveness and salvation, they talked about being filled with the Holy Spirit, but they didn't talk about Enlightenment.

It was probably sometime in middle school or high school in a world history class that I first heard of the concept. I didn't understand it, of course, and when I asked members of my family and church community about it, they talked about how dangerous it was to explore other religions and told me not to be tempted to turn my back on the Lord.

But, of course, I ignored them.

So what is Enlightenment?

Many people talk about the optimal human condition as Being in the Spirit, Becoming the Angel Within, The Beautiful State, Being In the Zone, In the Flow, etc.

But Enlightenment is far more than that.

It is Being Aware, and then Being the Awareness, in Silent Observance.

It is experiencing the Connectedness of all things, of being beyond self.

It is seeing that everything is AWESOME and AMAZING. It is waking up every day giving joyful thanks for another day of laughing and loving and sharing!

It is living in the moment, where Spirit grows within me with every breath, every heartbeat, every thought, every feeling, every sensation, and every experience.

It is about becoming not just a better version of myself, but being a completely new kind of Being.

And although I have tried to describe it many times, it is truly so beautiful, so incredible, so right that it defies description – it simply must be experienced.

And it is so COOL that everyone who experiences it just wants to experience it again and again, and then help everyone else experience it too.

How about you? Were you surprised to hear about Enlightenment the first time? Have you experienced it? How would you describe it?

TWO

The Evolution of Consciousness

My early religious training said that you were either in or out, saint or sinner, saved or not. There was no possibility of being part of the way there. That made being in the church really frightening to me – I was scared of making a fatal mistake and being condemned to hell for all eternity.

The church wanted to put the fear of God in me, and they were quite successful. Unfortunately, they put the fear of life into me, too. More on that later.

So I was surprised and delighted to learn about the Evolution of Consciousness, and that it was entirely possible to be partially and / or temporarily Enlightened. It was possible to make progress on the journey without completing the journey. And that took a lot of pressure off!

Over time I came to know that Being Enlightened is not a binary condition, like being pregnant or not – it's more like having a volume control knob that slowly moves and makes the sound louder or softer.

And here's the really great part of that: every step towards being in a completely Enlightened State is a glorious thing.

Being even a little bit more Loving, Peaceful, Wiser, Stronger, and Happier feels great!

And we can all celebrate every step towards a complete and permanent Awakening.

How about you? Do you see Enlightenment as a binary condition, where you are either there or you are not? Have you ever considered that Awakening could be a gradual process?

THREE
Awakening is a Skill!

Sometime after I learned about the Evolution of Consciousness, I began meditating. I meditated twice a day, once in the morning and another time after coming home from work. And over time, it became both easier and deeper. While I was focused on relaxing at first, after some time I began to experience Awakenings.

An Awakening, to me, is a sudden dramatic shift in consciousness that brings a higher level of Enlightenment. It brings more peace, joy, strength, wisdom, and love.

Sometimes an Awakening happens spontaneously or as the result of some triggering event. But in my case, it was a skill that I was developing.

What a wonderful surprise!

That's right, Awakening is a skill that can be practiced and developed just like learning to play tennis or learning to sing.

And every time we choose to have an Awakening moment, it not only pays off immediately – it pays off every day for the rest of our lives! As we develop the habit of Awakening, it becomes easier and easier to do.

How wonderful is that!

How about you? Do you see the pursuit of Enlightenment as a skill? Are you Practicing your Awakenings? Are they getting easier?

FOUR

Every Awakening is Surprisingly Wonderful!

Even after Awakening 50,000 times or more, I am always surprised at how powerful, loving, kind, peaceful, wise, and happy I am when I experience an Awakening and reach a higher vibration.

I am surprised at:

- How much I love people who are so different than me.
- What it is like to fall in love with everyone I meet.
- What it feels like to see everyone as a precious child – my very own precious child – and love them unconditionally.
- How wonderful it feels to be consumed by love and connected to all things.
- How amazing it is to look at someone and see / imagine all of the moments of their lives. To see them as an infant, a toddler, a young boy or girl, a young adult, a mature adult, and as an old man or woman. To see them on their death bed. To see all of their moods: their joy, sadness, anger, and love… to see the totality of their human experience. And to love everything I see.

Enlightenment isn't just indescribable, I also can't really remember what it feels like when I'm not there. I have to experience it again in order to really understand its depth and beauty. And each time I return, it is better than I expected or remembered it to be.

And the most amazing thing of all? Even when I think I have returned, even when my breath is taken away by the glory of it all, I discover that there is more: more Peace, more Joy, more Power, more Wisdom, and more Love.

I discover that I have been complacent, and that I have just scratched the surface of how indescribably wonderful Enlightenment can be.

> *How about you? Are your Enlightened moments better than you expected them to be? Are you amazed every time you return?*

FIVE
Anyone Can Become Enlightened!

Enlightenment is the potential we each have; everyone has the Greatness, Happiness, and Divinity within.

While most Awakened and Enlightened people have spent years of focused effort practicing and developing their Awakening skills, others have simply gone to bed one person, and woken up someone much different.

They had a spontaneous Awakening.

Contemporary examples include Byron Katie, Eckhart Tolle, and Adyashanti. Muhammad Subuh Sumohadi-widjojo (aka "Bapak", the founder of Subud), was enveloped by a white light and subsequently surrendered to the Power of the Universe. I am sure that there are many other examples.

So you never know who will "win the spiritual lottery" and become the next Enlightened, Awakened person.

It might be your friend, your spouse, or your son or your daughter. It could be the lady next door or the jerk in the hardware store.

And it could be you.

---

*How about you? Do you believe that you can become Enlightened?
Do you believe that anyone can?*

SIX

The Progression of Life

I am surprised that no one else is communicating the Progression of Life in the way that I do. Maybe no one else is tracking their progress in the way I have been tracking my progress every day for the past dozen years.

Life is full of ups and downs, but as we continue on our journey, I think that most people who are actively doing their inner work find that their average vibration increases over time. The highs are higher, and the lows aren't quite as low. And over time, the highs last longer and the lows don't last as long.

This is quite literally the most important figure in my life, and represents my actual experience, rating my positive energy day by day, over a long period of time:

It shows me the ups and downs of my days, with a trendline that is ever moving upwards.

It helps me stay humble when I have a really good day, and optimistic when I have one that's not so good.

It helps me to stay detached.

My guess is that you would see the same thing if you measured your positivity every day for years as I have.

Give it a shot!

How about you? Do you experience the same progression and ups and downs that I do? Are you moving steadily upward?

SEVEN

Few People are
Consistently Awakened

I am surprised that so few people are consistently Awakened. It is such a Beautiful Amazing Experience that I wonder why others don't see it, pursue it, and live it every day.

In truth, I am more than just curious, I am shocked!

I think the average person barely gets it. They have moments of joy, maybe a brief flash of Awakening, but I don't think they ever get to experience Spirit in its rich incredible beauty.

I wonder if I am one in a hundred, or even one in a thousand. Or more.

I am often in places with hundreds of other people – in an airport, or a movie theater, or a large store – where I think I may be the only one in that huge crowd experiencing the Beauty of the Spirit in that moment.

Happily, gratefully, and humbly, there are other times when I am in places where I feel like there are many in the room who are exuding a higher vibration than me in that moment. But those moments are rare, and are becoming rarer still.

And I am always grateful to be in the presence of those with a very high vibration, because there simply aren't enough of us.

Let me be clear: I want you to be Consistently Awakened, too. In fact, I want you to be even more Awakened than I am, so you can help me and others on our journey in your own special way.

Join us.

> *How about you? Are you surprised that so few people are consistently Awakened?*

EIGHT

Few People Are on The Path

I am surprised that there aren't more people on the path to the Enlightenment, and I often wonder why.

It must be that Enlightenment is hard to understand and believe.

I think that it must be that those of us who are blessed to live life at a higher vibration, try as we may, are not very good at sharing the beauty of the Spirit.

For example, very few parents tell their children about the Beauty of Enlightenment. They tell them that they have tremendous potential, that they can go to school and become a doctor, a lawyer, or even president, but they rarely tell them that they can become Enlightened.

And it appears that there are only a few religions and Spiritual communities led by truly Enlightened and Awakened people.

Unfortunately, it seems that some organizations really don't want their members to experience Enlightenment and be free – their system is designed to send the message that only a few of the elite members – the priests, preachers, elders, etc. – can achieve it or something close to it. The system is designed to maintain power and control over the masses.

I think the leaders often think they are doing their followers a favor, and perhaps they are for a while. But eventually, the path becomes a prison.

And there is a lot of confusion on terminology, and a lot of advice on the methods. Vegetarian? Vegan? Monastery? Abstinence? Tantra Yoga? Song and Dance? Silence and Stillness?

As they say in sales, "the confused mind won't buy"; and when it comes to Enlightenment, I think "the confused seeker won't seek." They just give up.

Gratefully, I never gave up. I just couldn't, because with every insight, with every surprise, I felt better. I felt stronger and safer and happier.

So how do we tell whether we are being led by someone of a high vibration, someone who is Enlightened? It's simple... truly Enlightened and Awakened people speak of Love and Connectedness. They do not put people down, they lift them up. They share their truth in a humble, kind, and loving way, instead of beating you over the head with it. They don't insist that you agree with them; instead, they offer their truth and wish you the best.

If more of our Spiritual leaders were like that, I think a lot more people would be on a path.

How about you? Are you on the path? Are you surprised that everyone isn't consciously and actively on a path, too?

NINE

Some People Don't Want or Need a Path

I've talked a lot about being on a path, but I was very surprised to learn that children and other beautiful people could just manifest Spirit on their own, without teachers and without a path!

How cool is that!

This drives some teachers and preachers crazy! And frankly, it took me a long time to accept it, too, because I was not one of those people. I needed and wanted a path.

I am blessed with many wonderful relatives and friends who are not actively or visibly pursuing Enlightenment or higher consciousness, but they are growing wiser every day, too. I can feel them making progress. As my love grows, their love grows, too.

Insights, Awakening, and Enlightenment can happen naturally and in a moment. So just because someone isn't on the same path as you, and even if they don't appear to be on any path at all, they are.

We all are.

How about you? Do you know any wise and happy people who seem to naturally be that way? Are you on a focused journey of Awakening, or are you just naturally becoming more Awakened and Enlightened every day?

TEN

Anyone Can Have an Enlightened Moment

I am often surprised when someone who doesn't seem to have a particularly high vibration has an Enlightened moment. They say something wise and loving, and in that moment, they are my teacher. Love and the Light comes through them as powerfully as it ever has come through anyone else.

It could be a friend or a partner.

It could be a child.

It could be that bombastic guy who is into conspiracy theories.

It could be you.

For example, a friend offered a bit of wisdom just a few weeks ago when he said: "I really don't think I eat too much... but apparently, I do!" It was an Awakened and humorous statement that both surprised and delighted me.

Now I look for those moments. I give people credit and honor the Spirit that flows through them, if only for a moment.

I honor the Wisdom and the Love, and by doing so, I encourage it to spring forth again.

So how about you? Have you been surprised when someone has an Awakened, Enlightened moment?

ELEVEN

You Never Know Where You Will Encounter an Enlightened Person

I am often surprised to discover an Enlightened, Awakened person in a place where I didn't expect it.

I expect to find them at a church, temple, or an ashram. I look for them at Spiritual gatherings, and often find them there.

But I have also found them at business events, at the gym, and on social media.

They could be sitting in the cubicle right next to you, or at the vegan restaurant, or at the barbeque joint on the other side of the railroad tracks.

And you might even find one at a grocery store. That's where I met Smitty, one of most positive, upbeat, Awakened people I have ever met. He was working the register, we were both just being Awesome, and now I look forward to shopping every week just so I can see him again.

And these days, I look for Awakened and Enlightened people everywhere.

And I find them!

How about you? Have you ever been delightfully surprised to find an Awakened person right in front of you?

TWELVE

We Don't Have to Struggle

I was surprised to learn that I didn't have to struggle.

Whether we choose to follow a proven, established path, or carve out our own, or seem to walk no path at all, we don't have to struggle.

Sure, it can be tough to face your fears and weaknesses. It takes a lot of courage to admit mistakes and to truly understand the power of the subconscious mind. But it doesn't have to be a struggle.

And at some point, we all need to let go of the fear and stress. We get to let go of the pain. We have the incredible blessing of stepping into peace and joy.

We can work hard, to be sure. A lot of things we want to do require focus and effort, but they don't require us to struggle.

In my world, effort + fear = struggle. Without the fear, there is just the effort, and that effort can be joyous!

We win by seeing life as a game to be played and watched, instead of a battle to be won.

We can let go, relax, release, and Surrender into Spirit. We don't have to struggle at all.

Surprise!

How about you? Are you struggling on your journey? Can you see the value and wisdom in letting go of that fear and enjoying the Road to Enlightenment?

THIRTEEN
How Easy Life Can Be

I was surprised to come to the point in my journey where, now, almost everything is easy. I just didn't see that coming.

This was such a revelation that I wrote a little book on this subject, too, called "The Easy Book". It contains a collection of insights on the subject.

Here's the first one:

It occurs to me that the only times life seems hard to me
  is when I am frightened and focused on large tasks

> And that by detaching and changing my focus to the next, simple task,

  life becomes easy.

Completing that next big project

> Starts with just sitting down at the keyboard,

> and that is easy.

That next book

> Starts with writing that first sentence,

> and that is easy, too.

The next hard workout

> Continues by taking that next breath,

> and that is easy.

The next step is always easy when the task is small enough.

Moment by moment,

> Focusing on the now

> > Life is Always Easy.

> *How about you? Have you discovered how easy life can be when you are in the Eternal Now?*

FOURTEEN

The Healing Power of Being Vulnerable

I was very resistant to being open to others and sharing my fears and I was surprised to find out how healing it can be.

It took me a lot of courage to be vulnerable, especially in front of other men. As a boy, I didn't dare to show any weakness and risk being seen as a sissy. That's because bullies pick on sissies and being vulnerable just wasn't safe at all.

And it sure was a struggle to pretend to be tough all of those times.

Finally, one day I was able to say "this hurts" and get the support I needed to admit and deal with the pain. It was a humbling experience.

Don't get me wrong, I know that sometimes "sucking it up" or "cowboying up" is the best thing to do in the moment, but it is also wise to take time to be vulnerable later.

Because it is only by discovering and sharing the pain that we can move through it. Being vulnerable and real is the only way to heal the inner pain.

And surprise! While vulnerability feels like weakness to me, it looks like courage to everyone else.

How about you? Are you able to be vulnerable and open up to others. Are you able to feel and share your pain?

FIFTEEN
Surrendering is a Superpower

I used to hate to think about surrendering, and I was surprised to learn how beneficial it can be. I was surprised to learn that surrendering is really a superpower!

I remember when a friend of mine encouraged me to embrace the power of surrendering and how resistant I was. To surrender was to admit defeat! It just wasn't something I was willing to do at all. Boys didn't give up! Men didn't yield! Only quitters and weak people surrendered!

I needed to win, and I needed to be in control. To come in second wasn't safe; to be a follower wasn't safe. So I resisted surrendering for a long time.

But then I gave it a shot. First, I relaxed, then I let go, then I Surrendered. And the peace and love and joy that came flowing over me and into me was incredible.

So now I Surrender many times a day. I let go of and release all my fears, desires, attachments, addictions, and limiting beliefs. I surrender my self-identity. I surrender everything. I free myself of any shadow energy, and all of the barriers between me and Spirit just vanish.

I Surrender and return to the Loving Awareness and the Silent Emptiness of the Eternal Now.

How about you? Are you able to surrender all of your fears and shadow energy?

SIXTEEN

The Nature of Truth

I was very surprised to learn about the nature of truth.

As children, we have little choice but to accept the truth of others... sitting on our mother's knee, learning in elementary school. The facts are shared, and we learn. But in addition to the facts, we also get perspectives, opinions, and beliefs, and having no filters or experience with which to validate them, we accept them as truth, too.

And it is a huge surprise to discover that our moms, dads, preachers, and teachers might be wrong about some things, or that the things they held as true were not universally accepted as truth. It can be very frightening to realize that we might be wrong about some things, too (much more on that later).

Over time, we learn to analyze the messages we receive, filtering them through our personal experience, our studies, and the reports of others. And still, we find that much truth is subjective and changes with the years.

One of the most surprising things I have learned is that there are many different kinds of truths – there are facts, perspectives, opinions, beliefs, judgements, viewpoints, conclusions, assumptions, definitions, ideas, theories, hunches, convictions, etc.

And a lot of people don't know the difference. They think their beliefs are facts, and when they do, they are very reluctant to change them.

After all, how can you change the facts?

How about you? Have you questioned the truths of the powerful people in your life? Do you truly think for yourself?

SEVENTEEN

The Fragility of the Human Mind

I was surprised to learn that most people have short circuits and are a little bit crazy. Some people are a whole lot crazy. Some very intelligent, highly rational people are crazy in some way, and for some of them, it is in a way that destroys the rest of their lives.

These include engineers, doctors, lawyers, entertainers, athletes, politicians, teachers, preachers, and moms and dads.

These people who are marvelously competent in many ways might be hoarders, they may be grossly obese, they may be addicted to substances (alcohol, drugs, etc.), or even be criminals in some way. They may be paranoid, schizophrenic, or have some other mental / emotional disorder. They have a flaw in their system that is destroying them, and in many cases, they just can't see it.

Some people's craziness isn't in what they do, they just have crazy beliefs: blindly attached to a religion, a cult, or a political party, never questioning them and having all their identity tied up in a group or a cause. They could believe in wild, paranoid conspiracy theories or end-of-the-world prophecies, so much so that it destroys their relationships and significantly damages a big part of their lives. They don't have the ability to see that they are wrong, or the courage or strength to admit that they are wrong, even when the facts are right in front of their faces.

In some cases, they disown their families or become estranged from those they love just because the group tells them have to do so in order to remain a member of the group. In other cases, the family and friends leave them, because they just can't deal with the craziness.

And in truth, it has always made me nervous to think that I might be one of those people. Seeing other people's insanity has caused me to question my own sanity many times, because I, too, believe some pretty crazy things.

And I suspect that all truly sane people question their own sanity somewhere on the Road the Enlightenment – and sometimes, they discover a little craziness and correct it.

How about you? Do you know any crazy people? Do you ever question your own sanity, too? Have you ever discovered a little bit of personal craziness?

EIGHTEEN
Biases and Blind Spots

I was surprised to learn about biases and blind spots – yours and mine. Everyone has them.

Biases occur when we are not completely objective. We have preferences that impact our judgement, and we are mostly unaware of them. They are formed when we are young and trying to make sense of the world and are mostly unconscious. We generalize, make some conclusions, and form biases without even knowing it. And then often, our confirmation biases simply don't allow us to see things that are contrary to our personal truth.

For example, when I was younger, I was a bit of a racist without even knowing it. I believed in the messages of the racist culture of my youth, and it took me years and a few very special experiences to wake up to the unconscious biases I was holding onto and then correct them.

Blind spots happen when we simply can't see things and don't know something is there - until, of course, someone points them out to us or we stumble upon a truth that has been at our feet the whole time.

And the biggest surprise about biases and blind spots? I still have them! You still have them, too. We all have them. I know that tomorrow I'll open my eyes and see something I have never seen before or see the same old thing in a new and different way. I know that I'll discover some hidden preconception or a preference that I didn't even know that I had.

I am humbled by my biases and blindspots, and I expect that you will be too.

And I wonder what I'll discover next.

How about you? Have you accepted the fact that you have biases and blind spots? Have you found a way to deal with them?

NINETEEN
Brainwashing

As surprised as I was to learn about biases and blind spots, I was even more surprised to learn that I have been brainwashed... and that we all have been brainwashed.

You see, we all form conclusions from the information we receive, giving special significance to those people who are certain and passionate, and often confusing repetition with truthfulness.

That's right – the subconscious mind can't tell the difference between truth and familiarity. So when we hear the same message many, many times, especially when those messages come with confidence and passion, we come to accept them as true.

When the "truth" comes from authority figures and caregivers in our lives, our parents, teachers, preachers, and leaders, and when they are accepted by a large number of people who surround us, they are given even more credence.

One of the hardest things to do is to make up our own minds when those who surround us all agree on some version of truth, and then repeat it over and over again, no matter how crazy it is.

But that isn't nearly as difficult as realizing that we have all been brainwashed in some way.

Surprise!

How about you? Do you understand how your opinions, beliefs, and convictions are formed over time by the passion, certainty, and frequency of the messages you have received?

TWENTY

Doubts, Criticisms, and Resentments

One of the most unpleasant surprises on the Road to Enlightenment was that some people simply didn't want to believe I was making progress on my Journey.

I am sure this is related to the fragility of the human mind, their own blindspots, and their need to be right, but more than anything, I think seeing another person making good progress can be a frightening thing. People often resent the success of others because it makes them feel weaker and somehow less lovable, themselves.

And if that person who is making progress is following a different path or spiritual system, then it is doubly frightening, because they may question the validity and effectiveness of their own path and belief system.

And so instead of praising the progress and supporting the work, they focus on the remaining imperfections. They may even say things like "you are being dishonest with yourself" or "you'll never make it, you should just give up", directly or indirectly.

As it turns out, how we respond to those who don't believe we are making progress, and those who seek to hold us back and in essence, want us to remain at a lower level, tells us a lot about the progress we have made and the work that remains.

If we are afraid or discouraged, if we resent their resentment, if we doubt ourselves because they doubt us, then we still have a strong need for approval and a fear of rejection.

On the other hand, if we respond with love, understanding, and compassion, we can celebrate a much higher vibration.

And if we are able to find some truth in their criticism and learn from it, if it just makes us more committed to our journey, well, then that's really special.

How about you? Have you experienced the doubts, criticisms, and resentments of others? How are you responding to them? Do you look for the truth in their criticism?

TWENTY-ONE
The Challenge of Remembering

Some things I remember quite well – phone numbers, math tables, songs, and poems – but remembering Spirit and how wonderful it is to be Awakened, well, that has proven to be surprisingly difficult to do.

I have experienced an Awakening, a shift of consciousness, perhaps 50,000 times over the past 50 years and have been distracted and forgotten just as many times.

It is one thing for me to shift into a High Vibration, and another thing to stay there. The habits of lower consciousness, especially my deepest fears, were so ingrained, so much of who I was, that it has taken decades to overwrite that programming.

And here's what I learned: the moment is very magnetic. It is very easy to get attached to the current experience, and then it is hard to Remember anything else. I think that staying focused and attached must somehow feel safer to my subconscious mind than Remembering and Shifting.

It's quite a humbling experience, but I'm getting used to it. It's getting easier and easier to Remember.

I wrote and recorded a 45-minute inspirational message once just to help me remember the important things. It was my first proven-to-work-every-time path to Awakening. I was my Magic Pill!

And of course, I called it "Remember".

How about you? Do you get distracted and forget about the Beauty of the Spirit, too? Do you have a proven way to help you remember?

TWENTY-TWO

The Subconscious Mind is in Charge

One of the biggest surprises for me was to learn that the subconscious mind is always in charge. I didn't want to accept it for a long time, because it was such a frightening concept!

You see, I took great pride in our ability to think – that being smart was a huge part of my self-esteem. My internal dialogue was what "I" was. My thoughts kept me safe and defined "me".

But we all have a lizard brain, and all of our sensory experiences pass through it first before they get to our rational, conscious brain. And the truth is that our subconscious mind is far more powerful than our rational, thinking mind.

The subconscious mind reacts first, reacts strongest, and is pretty much in control all the time. We make decisions emotionally and subconsciously, and then justify them rationally and consciously.

The subconscious is so powerful that in times of stress it simply takes over.

Salespeople know that. Every sales training program I have ever seen – and there have been a bunch of them – talks about how people make decisions emotionally and then justify those rationally. They rationalize their emotional choices.

But the conscious mind still thinks it knows what is going on, and that it is in charge. Surprisingly, neither is commonly true – the rational mind rarely understands that decisions are emotional, and it is in charge only when the subconscious mind feels safe and is at rest.

And it's not easy to discover what is going on in our subconscious mind. We discover what programs are running in our subconscious mind only by sitting in the silence or by looking objectively at our behaviors and our results.

And that can be scary. The discovery of "I am not who I thought I was" is always just a little frightening.

How about you? Were you surprised to learn that the subconscious mind was in control? Did it scare you, too?

TWENTY-THREE
The Law of Protection

Here's a big surprise that makes perfect sense when you think about it: the subconscious mind is the cornerstone of our survival mechanism and it takes over in times of stress. It wants to, *it has to*, protect us.

The subconscious mind draws conclusions and makes generalizations to deal with the massive amount of data coming its way. It rapidly decides what is important and safe and creates little programs / apps that it stores and runs continuously.

The Law of Protection states: "No matter how illogical, ill-conceived, or ineffective their attitudes and behaviors are, everyone is just trying to protect themselves. We are all just trying rescue ourselves from our own fear and darkness as best we can."

And we are most likely acting in a way that is consistent with our childhood survival strategies – doing those things that protected us, or seemed to protect us, when we were much younger.

We will often ignore evidence that indicates that our survival strategies are no longer effective and are no longer working at all. And we could have tremendous confirmation bias, seeing only the reasons to continue with our habitual attitudes and behaviors, and ignoring the reasons for change.

When we are relaxed, we can change those programs a little easier, but it is extremely hard to change a habit when we are afraid. It takes a lot of calming down in order to feel safe enough to change. And if we are naturally tense and nervous, changing habits can be really hard to do.

To alter someone's behavior or belief, you must make them feel safe in changing, or at least safer in changing than they would be in continuing to do what they are doing and think what they are thinking. Otherwise, it can take a massive amount of courage on their part to face their fears and make a change.

> *How about you? Have you learned that the reason anxious people don't change very easily is that they are afraid to change? That their subconscious mind is desperately hanging on to what it thinks to be true, in order to keep itself alive and safe?*

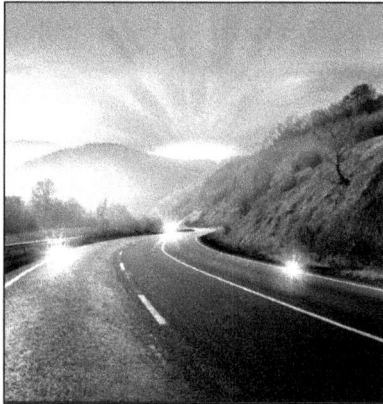

TWENTY-FOUR

Momentary Attachments

I am constantly surprised with how much I get attached to many of the moments in my life.

The thoughts, emotions, sensations, and experiences are so captivating!

I get attached to the games that I am playing, the shows I am watching, the conversations I am having, the stories I am telling myself, the thoughts that I am thinking, the feelings I am feeling, and yes, the words I am writing.

And I get REALLY attached to the moments when I am frightened or have a strong desire.

And even though I have experienced hundreds of millions of moments in my lifetime, I still get attached.

Then I wake up, let go, transcend, and return to Spirit.

Over and over and over again.

> *How about you? Do you still get attached, too? How long do you stay attached before you wake up again?*

TWENTY-FIVE
The Power of Habits

I was surprised to learn how powerful our attachments, habits, and addictions can be.

The subconscious mind is not only in charge, it is also stubborn as hell! Our habits are like ruts worn in the concrete, and it is very difficult to get out of a rut. Likewise, it is very difficult to replace an old, strong habit with a new one.

The subconscious mind doesn't want to change. It wants to be right. It *NEEDS* to be right and feel safe.

It takes willpower and repetition to replace ruts in the concrete of the subconscious mind. Unfortunately, willpower is an exhaustible resource: we only have so much of it, and when we get tired, the conscious mind, our willpower, usually rests and the subconscious mind takes over again.

Sometimes, as with severe drug addictions, it is literally impossible for people to change on their own. They get so far in the ditch that they can't pull themselves out at all, so they need to spend a lot of time in hospitals and treatment centers, and usually multiple times. They desperately hold onto their habits and addictions, even if they are causing incredible damage – even if they are sure to cause death.

So, we all need to choose our habits carefully. As Warren Buffet says: "The chains of habit are too light to be felt until they're too heavy to be broken."

But here's some really good news: we can all develop Habits of Higher Consciousness, too. With practice, we can develop the habit of being wise, loving, peaceful, powerful, and joyful people.

First, we try, then we practice, then we master, then we develop the habits, then what was once difficult becomes second nature, and we become a completely new person.

We can leverage the power of habits to our divine advantage!

How about you? Were you surprised to learn about the power of your habits? How are you at changing your habits?

TWENTY-SIX

Creativity and Rational Thought are Mutually Exclusive

I was very surprised to learn that the brain's center for wisdom and intuition and the brain's center for rational thought are (mostly) mutually exclusive.

Wow! That's why it is tough for "thinkers" to also be intuitive and emotionally sensitive at the same time.

That's why it is hard to be completely detached when doing "rational things", like computer programming, financial analysis, and technical writing.

This is the "left brain, right brain" meme that is so prevalent. Very few people are able to be active in both areas of the brain at the same time.

It could also explain why engineers, programmers, and accountants have a hard time with soft skills, like sales, customer service, and emotional intelligence.

It is easier to be very detached, relaxed, and intuitive during activities that don't require focused rational thought, such as walking, doing the dishes, dancing, yoga, singing memorized songs, playing silly games, sitting silently, etc.

I'm guessing that's why it's important to tame your rational mind and why they don't have technical writing and accounting as standard activities in monasteries. ☺

So how about you? Are you surprised to learn that rational thought and intuitive thought are nearly mutually exclusive?

TWENTY-SEVEN
The Challenge of Complacency

After I was successful at significantly reducing my fear, I was surprised to run into the challenge of complacency. It has absolutely been one of the toughest challenges on this Journey to Enlightenment.

I discovered that once I escaped the dangers of the jungle and found safety in my little cave, I didn't have a burning desire to grow anymore. I was safe, and I was good.

But staying in the cave was never going to help me make more progress!

I had to convince myself at a deep subconscious level that returning to Spirit many times a day was the safest and smartest thing I could do. I had to convince myself that leaving the safety of the cave was the best thing for me in the long run.

So I repeated this little mantra every day for months and months:

"It is Easy for me now to overcome my complacency. All I have to do is Remember that I am Safest, Strongest, Healthiest, and Happiest when I am In the Spirit and talking to others about Spirit, and that Awakening, Returning, and Focusing on Spirit are, by far, the Smartest things that I can do."

I was surprised at how long it took and delighted that it finally worked!

How about you? Are you trapped by complacency, or are you willing to courageously take the next step on your Journey?

TWENTY-EIGHT
The Need to Be Right

I was surprised to learn how much people need to be right. I was even more surprised to learn how much *I* needed to be right!

You see, being wrong is scary. It takes a lot of courage and strength to own up to a mistake or face a weakness. Because being wrong means that you had made a mistake, and being seen as one who makes mistakes puts you at a lot of risk of being shunned and rejected by the crowd.

Or so I thought.

So while I have seen a lot of people resistant to admitting a mistake or changing their mind, I have to admit that I was right at the top of the list.

I not only needed to be right, I needed to be the best! I needed to get an "A". I got pissed off when I gave the wrong answer or – heaven forbid! - got a "B"!

I didn't want to get a bad grade, be kicked out of the club, or fired from a job. I didn't want to be rejected, shunned, ostracized, excommunicated, condemned, or pushed away. I wanted to be right, and I wanted to be accepted and honored for my "rightness".

And I had a very hard time of seeing, much less accepting, my own craziness, my blind spots, and my mistakes.

I think most people have the same issues. When we are stressed out, we need to be right even more, and will defend our "truth" to the point of ridiculousness. That's especially true if we have declared our truth publicly or joined a community of fellow believers. Then changing our mind not only means courageously admitting that we made a mistake, it could also mean risking getting kicked out of the club, or worse, the family.

Most people have a hard time questioning their own truth, because at some deep subconscious level, they fear for their own sanity. I know I did.

But now that I have faced my own issues for so many years, it's getting a lot easier.

And that's great news!

With practice, it gets easier to question and revise your own truth

> *How about you? Do you really understand that the reason people don't even consider other possibilities is that they are afraid to consider them at a deep subconscious level? That they are afraid of making a mistake and afraid of getting kicked out of their community?*

TWENTY-NINE
The Need to Belong

I was surprised to learn how much people, including me, needed to belong to a community. The need for approval is so strong with most people that it can rightly be called an addiction and an instinct.

That's because we were all born helpless, instinctually seeking the acceptance, the approval, and the support of others. We needed to belong to a family and a tribe to survive. Without their support, we are quite literally, dead.

My addiction to approval was incredibly strong. For decades I thought that I just needed to be right, but then I discovered that what I wanted even more was to be seen to be right by others.

Getting good grades taught me that being right brought acceptance (and even applause!) from parents and teachers, and sometimes, the other kids.

Being right, being smart were a means to an end, and the end was being respected and accepted.

And I was far from alone: almost everyone has a strong tribal instinct and a powerful need to be accepted by others.

We need a family. We need a tribe. We need to belong.

How about you? Do you feel a strong tribal instinct? Do you need a family, close friends, and a tribe, too?

THIRTY
There's a Tribe for Every Truth

Some beliefs, practices, and people are just plain crazy (see The Fragility of the Human Mind, above), and surprisingly, no matter how crazy they seem to be, powerful people can always gather a tribe around them.

That's usually how cults are created and maintained. Some crazy but powerful person (usually a man) declares that he has some mysterious divine truth or power, and if he repeats the claim strong enough and often enough, he will gather a tribe.

A tribe of like-minded people, or simply, a tribe of those looking for someone to follow, gathers around the certainty.

Usually, the cults / tribes have some great practices that provide significant value for the tribe. They have ceremonies, great music, and wonderful gatherings of all kinds. But mostly they have a lot of sensitive people who want to belong to a community and a family, and who take care of each other once they are in that community.

That's how much people want to belong to a community. They are willing to forego logic and reason to be a part of a tribe. They are literally willing to be crazy and then refuse to question their own craziness, just to be in that tribe. They are willing to be violent and to justify their violence in whatever way they can, just to be in that tribe.

Skeptical? The flat earth society and any number of other doomsday prophets are still among us, gathering and rewarding their tribes, even today.

How about you? Are you surprised at the craziness of some communities? Is your tribe a little crazy, too?

THIRTY-ONE

The Power of Independence

I was surprised to learn about how powerful it can be to be independent.

Claiming your own truth without needing anyone to agree with you is simply AWESOME!

Being able to be cool, calm, and collected when others are frightened and/or combative is a true gift.

And seeing each moment as independent of all other moments is the ultimate freedom.

Wonderfully, being independent, like so many other things, is a skill that can be mastered. It just takes courage and practice.

So try these techniques when it comes to being independent of others:

- Practice putting your shields up. Imagine that an impenetrable, transparent barrier between you and other people exists. Imagine that no matter what, nothing they can say or do will ever reach you.

- Practice seeing yourself as being made of rubber, and such that all the toxic energy that comes to you simply bounces off.

- Practice seeing yourself as ethereal, such that the toxic energy simply passes through you, like wind passing through a screen door or the wind passing through the leaves of a very large tree. It comes in, has no or very little impact, and then it is gone.

And try these things for being in the moment:

- Put boundaries around this moment, turning it into a little room of its own. The past is in another room, the future is in another room that you will get to in just a minute, but for now, you are in the room of the moment.

- Or you can do something physical. Take a walk, take some deep breaths, sing a song, etc. Put an intermission in the play and get ready for the next act. Be in the intermission.

So let me repeat: seeing each moment as independent of all other moments is the ultimate freedom.

Try it.

How about you? Are you independent or dependent on others? Can you let go of the past, stop thinking about the future, and live in the moment?

THIRTY-TWO
Teaching the Inner Child

I was really surprised to discover how effective it is to talk to myself as if I was a child. I tried a lot of "college thoughts", but when it came to overcoming my deepest and strongest fears, desires, and limiting beliefs, I had to learn to work with my inner child.

That's because the subconscious mind, the limbic brain, is very much like a child. The deeper the programming, the simpler the language needs to be, because the inner child created the programming, and that child only understands very simple phrases.

So whenever I feel a little stress, I find myself saying things like:

- This is easy, this is fun, and I am strong
- I am safe, perfectly safe, and no one can harm me
- I am brave, I am strong, and I can do this!
- I'm OK right now and I have faith in the future.

There are hundreds of combinations and simple sequences of words that I can use, and sometimes single words work, too, words like "Love", "Easy", "Gentle", or "Patience".

Sometimes I run for miles and miles, or exercise for hours just repeating "Easy, Gentle, Safe, and Strong" to myself over and over again.

It takes some humility to speak to yourself that way, but surprisingly, it really works!

How about you? Have you tried speaking to yourself as if you were a child?

THIRTY-THREE
Controlled Thought

I was very surprised to learn how difficult it was to control my thoughts, and then how wonderful and powerful life was when I was finally able to do it.

When I started, 10 seconds of silence was the best that I could do. 10 torturous seconds.

My mind was racing all of the time, with multiple simultaneous, angry rants. Thinking about how someone was unfair, about what I should have done, and what I was going to do.

Then I learned to replace some angry and disempowering words with kinder, more empowering ones. I learned to say and think the word "eager" instead of the word "anxious". I learned to say "concerned" instead of "worried". I stopped "shoulding" on people and learned to suggest or offer instead of telling them they should do something or should think in a particular way.

Then I learned to slow down my thoughts. It took some edge off of them by simpler thinking more slowly.

Then I learned to speak to myself in a kind and loving voice, much like I would speak to the most precious little baby in the world.

And once I mastered controlling my thoughts, it was far easier to leave them behind and enter into the silence, even to the point of the spontaneous silence.

And here's one of my favorite sayings:

"Our thoughts can be our cruel masters, imprisoning, enslaving, and even torturing us in the dungeons of our own minds. Once controlled, however, they can become our faithful servants and trusted guides, leading us to the doorway of Heaven itself, where we must leave them behind and enter in silence."

How about you? Can you control the thoughts you think, and replace the harmful, disempowering ones with those that move you to Enlightenment?

THIRTY-FOUR
Sequences of Thought and Action

I was very surprised to learn that could shift my energy any time I wanted and get to a much higher state of consciousness if I just took it step by step.

And I was equally surprised that almost no other meditative techniques used the approach of purposeful intentions combined with incremental steps to shift energy.

Because of my background in computer programming and project management, defining the steps it took to achieve a task seemed perfectly normal to me – it was in my bones, really. You break down a large project into achievable tasks, and then you complete them one at a time.

You eat the elephant one bite at a time. You climb a ladder or walk up a staircase instead of trying to leap 20 feet in the air at once.

So I thought to apply the technique of incremental, small steps to shifting energy and I created Mind Sequencing, a process of shifting my state of being through purposeful intentions and sequences of thoughts and actions.

Perhaps no other spiritual teachers were software engineers and project managers in a previous life. ☺

How about you? Have you ever taken on a big project by breaking it down into a series of achievable steps? Have you tried Mind Sequencing?

THIRTY-FIVE

Peace of Mind

I had heard of having Peace of Mind for many years, and I was amazed and surprised to learn how incredible it feels to sit in the silence and experience it.

My journey started with full-body relaxation, which is a great place for everyone to start.

After I learned to relax my body, I learned to relax my thoughts. I learned to let go of my attachment to the moment. I learned to let go of my fear.

And a few years ago, I began to experience the spontaneous silence. I began to have true peace of mind. I was out walking my dog one day, and suddenly, my thoughts just stopped. They were replaced by a combination of silence and gentle, loving whispers. It was true Peace of Mind.

Now, I experience True Peace of Mind many times a day, and on some days, almost all of the time.

And it really is a surprisingly healing, empowering, and wonderful experience!

How about you? Have you experienced the Spontaneous Silence? Do you have Peace of Mind?

THIRTY-SIX
Inner Diversity

While superficial differences (like skin color, size, language, clothing, etc.) are obvious, inner differences are still surprising to me.

I'm analytical and organized. I make lists, write programs, and conceptualize.

But those things are difficult if not impossible for some people. Some people are just impulsive and shoot from the hip. Others just want someone else to make the decisions and then hand them a list of things to do.

I experience a wide range of emotions and think of myself as being sensitive and quite emotional. Other people may not be very emotional at all or seem to have a very limited range of emotions.

I think in words, as if someone in my head is talking to me. Some people think a lot (or mainly) in pictures. Some people don't have any inner narrative or any inner movie at all!

It's easy to see that children think and feel differently from adults, but I can't just look at an adult and see how they think differently and feel differently from other adults.

There are all kinds of tests we can take to determine our psychological type or "style": the Myers-Briggs, the DISC profile, MMPI, etc. come to my mind, and they help us to be aware of and appreciate the differences of our inner diversity.

But I am still often surprised when I run across an adult who thinks and feels so much differently than I do.

How about you? Have you taken any profiling surveys? What is your psychological type? What does your inner mind say and do?

THIRTY-SEVEN

Rudeness is Not True Power

I was surprised to learn that people who are rude and combative are trapped in their warrior energy, and they have a long way to go on their journey to enlightenment. When I was young, I thought that all the powerful people were also the ones to be most admired, but boy was I wrong about that!

As we make progress on our journeys, being able to be a fierce warrior is but a phase we must pass through; it is not a place to stay, although, unfortunately, many people get stuck there.

It is quite a paradox that letting go is an essential skill on the journey, and that angry responses to fear and stress keep us from becoming more powerful.

Letting go, it seems, is a more advanced level of power than being an angry and abusive warrior!

For a long time, I confused rudeness and anger with strength. But they are really indications of pain and fear. They are really signs of weakness.

Enlightened people are grounded, centered, and balanced. They are comfortable in their own skin.

They don't need to fight, and they don't need to win. They build people up instead of putting them down. They have great kindness, empathy, and compassion.

They have discovered that Love is a lot more powerful than anger.

How about you? Do you have any rude and combative people in your life? Do you see that they are really frightened and weak underneath?

THIRTY-EIGHT
Levels of Positive Energy

I was surprised to discover the Levels of Positive Energy. It was not something that was ever taught in my home, church, or school. There were conversations about being in a good mood or bad mood, but that was it.

Now, I see some very definite levels of consciousness, as follows:

Meta-Level	Level	Attributes
The Spirit	The Angel	Love, peace, bliss, serenity, joy, wisdom, enlightenment, oneness; focused on loving and being
	The Master	Gratitude, abundance, humility, confidence, service, productivity; focused on sharing and doing
The Transition	The Seeker	Trust, forgiveness, acceptance, openness, release, optimism; focused on learning, accepting, and understanding
	The Warrior	Courage, boldness, action, energy, decisiveness, focus, manipulation; focused on changing the internal and external worlds
The Pit of Darkness	The Prisoner	Regret, guilt, fear, desire, frustration, anxiety, stress, anger; focused on escape
	The Victim	Shame, apathy, depression, passiveness, weakness, vulnerability; focused on survival

At the **Victim Level**, someone is caught up in the emotions of shame, guilt, apathy, depression, passiveness, unworthiness, or humiliation. They feel weak. They are not focused on Doing, and their thoughts are stressful. There is very little vision or intention, and no detachment. They feel powerless and want to be left alone. They are focused on survival.

At the **Prisoner Level**, someone is still caught up in their emotions, but heavy into thoughts of escape and injustice. They have formed a Vision and an Intention of being free from their current situation. They feel trapped instead of feeling powerless, and they just want to escape, or they just want someone to rescue them.

At the **Warrior Level**, they have stepped into their Power and they are passionately doing things, either angrily or joyfully. They have a strong Vision and an Intention for the future, with great desires and needs. They exert energy and seek to manipulate and control their external and internal worlds. They seek to improve their condition by changing their situation and by transforming themselves.

At the **Seeker Level**, they are not so much focused on transforming themselves as they are on Watching and Learning. They have a strong Vision of their future and much less emotion than at the previous levels. They seek Peace and Wisdom through Understanding and Acceptance of themselves and others.

At the **Master Level**, they are focused on their Vision for the moment and the future. Their detachment is much greater, and they are able to Do, Think, and Feel with great effectiveness, all in service to the Vision that they are holding and to others, and without attachment to the outcome. They no longer feel driven to change others or themselves because they are no longer filled with desire. They are focused on sharing and doing.

And finally, at the **Angel Level,** they are less into Doing, Thinking, and Feeling, and more focused on just Watching and Being One with Presence. Their thoughts are quiet and fleeting, and their emotions are very subdued. At the Angel level, life is simply about Being, Watching, and Loving.

> *How about you? Do you recognize levels of positive energy in yourself and in others?*

THIRTY-NINE
The Effort Curve

I was surprised to discover that when I was at a lower level of positive energy, it was much harder to shift my vibration upwards than when I was at a higher level of positive energy.

When at the lowest levels, it is very hard to make any progress forward because the subconscious mind, in its deep fear, becomes very attached to what is. After all, it has chosen the current thoughts and feelings in a valiant attempt to protect itself, and it won't easily change its mind.

It is even hard to conceive that there ever was or possibly could be anything but the darkness in which someone finds themselves, and at some level, has chosen to continue. It is hard to remember the Love and the Light, and impossible to see it or feel it when you are at the lowest levels of energy.

Graphically, here's what it looks like:

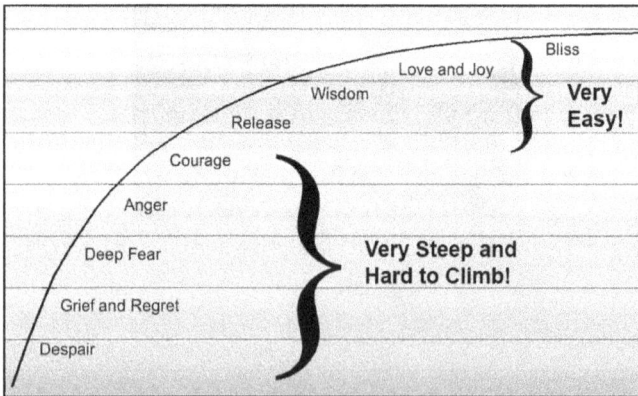

At the lowest levels, making progress is like climbing up a cliff. It is a technical climb, as with pitons, ropes, and partners. Very few people can climb up that cliff on their own.

At the top, making progress is a walk in the park. It's easy and enjoyable. When you are feeling great, it is easy to feel even better!

So if you are stuck, consider that you might be at a little lower level of positive energy than you thought that you were.

How about you? Do you see how hard it is to move upwards when you are deep in the pit of darkness? Where are you right now?

FORTY
Moving Between the Levels

Later, I was delighted to learn that there are surprisingly easy ways to help someone move up the levels of positive energy. The key is to move through them up one level at time.

When someone is experiencing Victim Energy, I help them see that they are not powerless, rather, they are just in a bad place. It helps them move up to the Prisoner Energy.

When someone is caught up in their Prisoner Energy, I help them see that they are not really trapped, and that they have the power to break free. That helps them move up to the Warrior Energy.

When someone is caught up in their Warrior Energy, I help them see that they don't need to keep fighting, that they can let go, and trust, and have faith. It helps them move up to the Seeker Energy.

When someone is caught up in their Seeker Energy, I help them see that they already have the power to help others and that they can make a real difference in this world with the power they already have. It helps them move up to the Master Energy.

And when someone is at the Master Energy Level, they are not likely to be caught there at all. All I have to do is remind them that the Angel Level awaits, and they are there.

> *How about you? Are you surprised to learn that there are simple ways to help someone reach a higher level of consciousness?*

FORTY-ONE

Beautiful People
Aren't Always Beautiful

I used to think that movie stars always looked like they were ready for the camera or stage, and that wealthy people were always happy, and that fame ensured lifetime success.

I think that's because when I was young, those were the messages I got from TV and, indirectly, from my family and community. They thought that beauty, wealth, and fame were the most important things in life, or at least close to it.

But, it's just not true.

I was surprised to learn that wealthy and famous people had marital problems. The first time I remember being surprised over that was when John Elway got a divorce. He was wealthy, famous, smart, and darn good looking. And he was a tall athlete, which is something I always wanted to be and never will be.

So, somehow, down deep, I thought his life was perfect. Then he got a divorce. And then, so did Tony Robbins. And a lot of other famous, wealthy, and beautiful people. Robin Williams even committed suicide, and so on.

Surprise! Beautiful people aren't always beautiful. Wealthy people aren't always happy. Famous people long for privacy and downtime, and a whole bunch of people who seem to have it all together are addicted to drugs and alcohol.

Some are far more stressed out and challenged than they let on. There can be a lot of tears behind the mask. There can be a lot of dysfunction and anger behind closed doors. There can be lots of health problems, addictions, family issues, etc. Great actors are really good at pretending that all is well.

And they have a hard time admitting to themselves, much less to others, that they have a problem. They don't want their public image to be damaged, because it can cost them dearly to be "real".

All too often, they hurt so much that they self-destruct. They engage in dangerous activities, especially drug use, and they can destroy themselves.

I think their success and focus on their careers has limited their focus on the other areas of life. They just pay attention to what is working for them, and their development in other ways is stunted.

That's what many coaches and counselors focus on living a balanced life. And the bottom line is that if you don't focus on creating a balanced life, you won't have a balanced life, and it will come back to bite you.

There are many forms of wealth. Having money in the bank, or being famous, are just a couple of them.

How about you? Were you surprised to learn that beautiful people aren't always beautiful? In what ways are you wealthy?

FORTY-TWO

Counselors and Preachers Don't Always Have It Together Either

I was surprised to learn that psychologists, counselors, therapists, and preachers often have their own emotional and mental health problems.

Many are not as loving, peaceful, and wise off-stage as they are on-stage or when they are in session, caring for others. Many have days or months of despair and depression even while they are doing their best to help others.

The truth is that every counselor, therapist, preacher, priest, teacher, etc. is still on their journey, too. They are still learning and growing, and still dealing with their own stresses. Many psychologists and counselors went into their profession, at least at some level, to work on themselves. Some televangelists seem to be either crying or angry all the time, even as they are doing their best to help others.

And their professions, while tremendously rewarding at times, can be incredibly stressful. Dealing with people who have a lot of toxic energy can be emotionally draining and damaging. So they are not only dealing with their own personal stress, they are dealing with other's stresses, too. And that can really add up.

When you wonder how they can be helping others while they are still on their journey, consider this: it's far easier to see the problems that other people have than it is to be honest with ourselves and see our own.

It is far easier to give good advice than it is to follow it.

> *How about you? Have you ever known a caregiver, counselor, therapist, or preacher who still had a lot of work to do?*

FORTY-THREE
Humility and Confidence Go Hand in Hand

I was surprised to learn that strong people can be humble, and even more surprised to find out that humility and confidence can grow together.

I used to think that strong, confident people were tough and arrogant. And I was surprised to learn that arrogance and egotism were the masks that insecure people wear, to keep people from seeing their fear.

Unfortunately, the mask of arrogance also keeps the wearers of the mask from seeing their own fear, too.

And as I continued to work on myself, I was surprised to learn that the more humbled and surrendered I became, the more I accept my weaknesses, mistakes, and shortcomings, and the more confident and powerful I became. The cycle looks like this:

- Confidence leads to courage
- Courage allows me to be honest with myself and see the opportunities for growth
- Humility allows me to accept what I see

- Learning allows me to grow
- Growth leads to more confidence.

And now I know that truly wise people are also truly humble people, too.

> *How about you? Do you see how confidence and humility go hand in hand?*

FORTY-FOUR
The Person We Can Become

I was surprised to finally learn that there is this incredibly beautiful person inside of everybody, shielded and disguised by layers of fear.

In my earlier days, I only saw people for who they were in the moment and I didn't really see their potential.

I'm sure that was because I didn't really see my potential, either. Sure, I knew that I could go to college, get a good job, earn some money, buy a house, etc. I saw what I could do and what I could have, but I never really saw the person I could become.

Now, I see that each of us has a Radiant Angel inside, trying to both wake up and stay safe. This Angel is filled with Peace, Joy, Strength, Wisdom, and Love. This Angel is confident, playful, powerful, and free.

And the Angel in you wants to come out and play with the Angel in me!

Coming to know this makes a world of difference.

How about you? Do you really see the person you could become? Have you discovered The Angel Within?

FORTY-FIVE
Our Incredible Power

I was very surprised to learn of the incredible power that we all have.

I used to focus on physical and mental power only. I loved being able to run fast and wrestle with kids my size (which was pretty darned small) and I reveled in the power of my physical body.

But mostly, I focused on the power of my mind to memorize things and solve problems. I used to be pretty darn smart, and being clever became an obsession.

It took me a while to start focusing on emotional power and spiritual power – the power of Beingness and Presence in all of its forms.

And we all have this incredible power:

- The power to Learn and Grow and Transform
- The power to Shift our Energy, Change our Perspective, and Raise our Vibration
- The power of Belief
- The power of Vision
- The power of Clarity
- The power of Focus and Attention
- The power to Improvise, Adapt, and Overcome.
- … and so on.

And usually all it takes to tap into this power is to believe that it exists.

How surprising is that!

How about you? Have you tapped into your power? Do you truly believe in yourself?

FORTY-SIX

The Power of Encouragement

I am often surprised, even to this day, about the power of Encouragement and Support.

You see, we each have the incredible ability to share Love and Light with each other, and it can make a huge difference in a person's life.

We all need reminding of who we can be, and we all need a little assistance out of the shadows from time to time. We need a shelter in the storm. We need a ladder to help us climb out of the pit of darkness.

And when we get that support, it is surprisingly beautiful.

And surprise(!) - when we give encouragement and support, it is beautiful, too! As we share messages of hope, we receive them, too. As we share wisdom, we are reminded of wisdom. The positive energy flows into us and through us, and nurtures us as we use it to nurture others.

And the more Love and Joy we share, the more Love and Joy we have.

What an incredibly wonderful surprise!

How about you? Have you been blessed with encouragement and support today? Have you been blessed to share it with others?

FORTY-SEVEN

The Power of Imagination

It has often been said that the subconscious mind can't tell the difference between imagination and reality, and while I don't think that that is completely true, I am often surprised at the power of my imagination.

If we imagine someone cutting a fresh, ripe lemon into quarters and then taking one of the sections and quickly biting into it so that a lot of lemon juice pours into our mouths, our imagination will most certainly cause our mouths to water.

If we imagine how incredibly wonderful it would be to win the lottery, we can for at least a few moments, experience the ecstasy of that incredibly good fortune.

If we imagine what it is like to be confident, firm, brave, and bold, we are transformed into a more powerful version of ourselves.

And more vividly we describe the experience, the more impact it will have.

Some say that whatever we visualize in incredible detail, with sufficient repetition and passion, will surely come to pass.

Some even say that if we imagine the Angels speaking to us and appearing before us, that they will. Most certainly, some people do seem to imagine such things, and then believe completely that it is true.

And there is a lot of evidence to suggest that we can manifest anything that we desire, simply by leveraging the power of our imagination.

How about you? Have you been leveraging the power of your imagination to transform yourself and manifest your heart's desire?

FORTY-EIGHT

The Addictiveness of Toxic Energy

It was a huge surprise to learn how addictive toxic energy can be. Fear is not only contagious, it is sought after and embraced by many people.

You see, fear is a stimulant. When we are frightened, the adrenaline starts pumping just like it does when we are excited. And it is the adrenaline that is addictive.

Unfortunately, fear and stress are harmful to us. They are toxic because stress really does kill. Heart attacks, strokes, high blood pressure, and a wide variety of deadly conditions can be traced back to stress.

Even more unfortunately, stressed out people often want others to be frightened, angry, upset, and worried, too... because it both justifies and validates their own feelings, and the adrenaline that others are pumping just adds fuel to everyone's fire. In the worst cases, it leads to mob behavior that leaves rationality and honor far, far behind.

Being in the toxic energy of a crowd can make someone feel safer, because they don't feel alone, and they feel validated and "right". They get permission from others to revel in the toxic energy and the adrenaline rush.

But here's the good news: positive energy and the rush of adrenaline that comes with it is addictive, too. The adrenaline that comes from positive excitement is both healthy and healing.

Let's share that instead.

Flipping the Switch

I was quite surprised to learn about the power we all have to "flip the switch" and shift our consciousness both dramatically and instantly.

This human experience is amazingly variable, with its agony and ecstasy often separated by only a few seconds.

Babies rapidly shift quite naturally. They can be crying up a storm, but if you get them to change the focus of their attention for just a second, they can stop it in an instant.

The same is true for adults. Many still have quite a temper, and you never know what will set them off. And some of us have developed the skill of instantly shifting in a positive way.

I remember hearing a story from a speaker who related that he was once having a loud and angry argument with his wife when the phone rang and interrupted the fight. Without thinking, he answered cheerfully and said "hello". And in that moment, he realized the power he had to "flip the switch" and shift his energy in an instant.

I think we have all done that.

And on a much grander scale, having a Salvation Experience, where you release all your anger, regret, resentment, and fear, and embrace forgiveness for all the mistakes you have made and the crap you have done, can "flip the switch" in a far deeper and stronger way.

All we have to do is Remember the Light and Believe in the Light, and the switch is flipped automatically.

How about you? Have you ever Flipped the Switch? Do you practice Flipping the Switch? Can you Flip it right now?

FIFTY
There is Always a Way

I remember the times that I have been around people who felt hopelessly trapped in their circumstance and how challenging it can be to get them to see that there is always a path out of the darkness. There is always a door or a portal to another reality.

And I've been there a few times myself, and then Surprise! I found a way out of the shadows, and most of the time, it was quite simple and right there in front of me.

You never know who is going to suddenly find a path through the darkness and out of their misery.

Burning bush moments, struck by lightning moments, and/or cracked-open moments can happen to anybody, any time.

So if you or anyone around you gets stuck in the darkness, just remember this: Surprise! There is always a way.

How about you? Have you ever been surprised with how easy it was to break free of the darkness and return to the light? Have you been surprised at how easily other people can do it?

FIFTY-ONE

How Frightened and Sensitive I Was – and Still Am!

It has been so very surprising to me that even after over 50 years of working on myself, I still have my moments of hesitation, resistance, and grumpiness. I usually get a few buzzes every day. They mostly go away as quickly as I become aware of them, but they just keep coming.

I even have an occasional moment of anger. Now, they are almost always small little flashes that only last a second or two, and I almost never speak harshly to someone or lash out in any way. I keep track of them all and I reflect on what triggered me and why I got angry, and that helps me learn more about myself.

But I thought I would achieve permanent Enlightenment long before now and I that would have come to that place where I never experience fear of any kind.

But not yet… not yet.

I keep exploring my fears and analyzing them, seeking to understand why they exist and how they were developed. Layer by layer, I am peeling the onion.

And fortunately, these days I am able to peel the onion without crying. Mostly, I am just surprised. ☺

How about you? Are you in touch with your fears? Have you analyzed them? Do you know why you have them and where they originated from?

FIFTY-TWO

How Much I Longed for Approval,
Acceptance, and Love

I am still surprised at the depth of my addictions to Approval, Acceptance, and Love from others.

Every time I peel back the onion a bit, I discover a deep desire to be Protected, Connected, Guided and Loved.

I'm pretty sure it comes from being a baby and getting relief from my mother and other caregivers. I was totally dependent. I needed rescuing.

Later, I wanted to get the top scores, finish first, and get the applause.

I think nearly all of us have these needs, desires, and addictions, unless we were abused and shunned by those from whom we sought affection. Attachment disorders and anti-social personality disorders impact a very small percentage of people.

The rest of us still appreciate a little Support, Approval, Compassion, and Respect from time to time.

How about you? Have you explored the depths of your need for approval from others?

FIFTY-THREE

How Much Pain People Can Endure

I've experienced a fair amount of pain in my life – I think everyone has. But some have experienced a lot more pain than others.

Sometimes the pain is unchangeable. A back problem, a hip problem, or some other sort of serious medical condition can cause such pain that a person has to be constantly medicated, and there is little or nothing that they or anyone else can do about it. I am surprised at how much of that kind of pain a person can endure.

And I was surprised to learn how often people continue to endure their pain even when it seems that they could make a simple choice to end it.

Such is the power of addictions, both the obvious ones (drugs, alcohol, tobacco, etc.), and the hidden ones (limiting beliefs, the fear of rejection, the fear of admitting a mistake, the fear of change, etc.)

The subconscious mind is surprisingly strong when it comes to holding onto patterns of thought and behaviors that it thought would keep it safe.

One of most insidious things it does it does is cling to the thoughts that "Change is dangerous! Don't do it! We are in pain now, but it could be worse if we changed!"

When someone is really frightened, deeply frightened, their fear will be greater than the pain that they have until they hit rock bottom and they just can't take it anymore.

Then and only then will they be open to change.

How about you? Do you know someone who is in an incredible amount of pain? In some way, are they continuing to experience that pain by choice? Is that someone you?

FIFTY-FOUR

Stress Often Goes Unnoticed

I was surprised to learn that some really stressed out and angry people don't think that they are stressed out and angry. They think of themselves as "normal". They can't tell how much pain they are in. Have no idea what peace of mind feels like. And they may even think that they are being realistic or positive in their outlook.

We humans have the most amazing ability to filter out information that we don't consider important. So pain and stress, when there is enough of it, simply becomes background noise. It gets ignored.

I am reminded of a dream I had in which an Angel appeared to me as a robust and healthy older man. He and some helpers held me down on my bed and took off my shoes. They didn't say anything; they just simply and lovingly held me down and took off my shoes. The relief was immediate. I had no idea that my shoes were on so tight, and that they were causing me so much pain and stress.

And I reflected throughout the rest of the day: how many times such a simple act of relieving stress – shifting my posture, letting go of an unhealthy, unloving thought or idea, letting go of a limiting belief – could make such a huge difference in my life.

And I wondered how many times I chose to suffer without realizing it. I wondered how many times I could have simply and quickly moved from a place of darkness and pain into a place of Light and Joy.

How about you? Do you know anyone who is in such tremendous stress and pain that they hardly even notice it anymore?

FIFTY-FIVE

The Mind-Body-Spirit Connection

This is going to sound weird, I know, but I was really surprised to learn that there really is an incredible connection between Mind, Body, and Spirit. I used to be so lost in my thoughts that I didn't think my body had anything to do with my mood.

And it generally didn't, because I was in a crappy mood almost all of the time, whether I was hungry and tired, or filled and well rested. So there was a very weak relationship between the mind and the body for me.

Now, there is much more of a connection, because I am so much more sensitive to how fatigue, hunger, and thirst can contribute to fear. And I am much more aware about how integrated and related the mind, body, emotions, and Spirit really are. I am much more aware of the Layers of Self and the importance of Energetic Integrity.

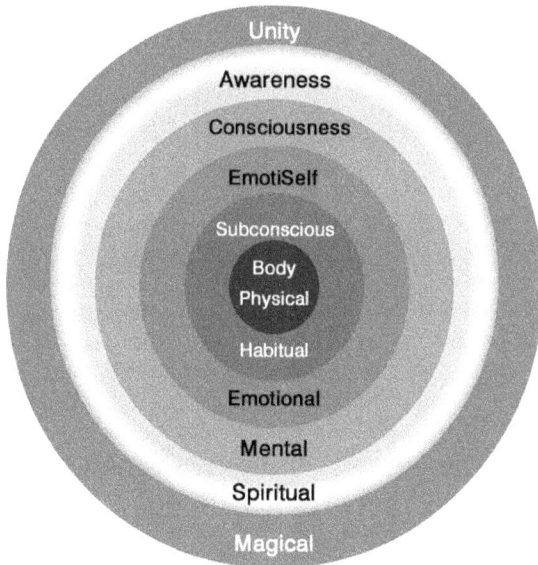

So now every time I choose to shift my energy and let go of a little bit of stress, which happens almost immediately after I notice that I have it, I always start with adjusting my body. My favorite technique is a simple one: Align, Breathe, and Smile.

First, I Align: I shrug my shoulders, roll my neck, wiggle a bit, and sit or stand up straight and tall.

Then I Breathe: I take just a few reasonably deep breaths and exhale powerfully to clear out all of the old energy.

Then I Smile: I think of something happy and celebrate some aspect of life.

Align, Breathe, and Smile. Try it right now!

So how about you? Have you discovered how helpful it is to first shift your body, and then shift your thoughts to effect a shift in your Spirit?

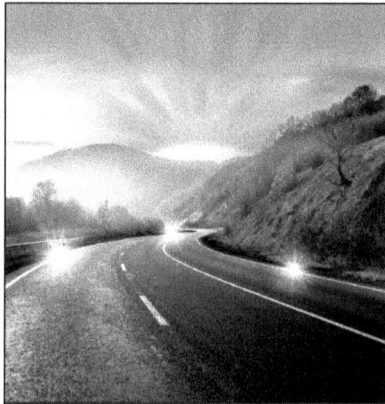

FIFTY-SIX

The Spiritual Body

I was surprised to see that many of the aspects of the physical body are appropriate to the emotional / spiritual self, too:

- We need healing when we are injured. It takes time, and treatment is really helpful, like going to a hospital or taking medication.

- For our physical body, we need rest, exercise, and nourishment

- And we can grow stronger with proper nutrition, exercise, and rest, and we grow weaker without it.

And our emotional / spiritual selves are often far more sensitive than our physical selves. Ideally, we would give ourselves emotional and spiritual nourishment more often than our physical bodies.

Shifting energy can be quick like grabbing a snack, or it can be extensive, like preparing and consuming a large meal:

- First, we have awareness of hunger or thirst

- Then we decide what nourishment we want or need

- Then we prepare the meal

- Then we set the table

- Then we consume the meal.

So with thoughtful, practiced energy shifting techniques, such as Mind Sequencing, we develop the habit of nourishing our emotional and spiritual selves frequently throughout the day. Ideally, we consume energetic, emotional, and spiritual nourishment whenever and wherever it is needed, via:

- **Scheduled** nourishment (e.g., morning practice, scheduled prayers, or meditation)

- **Responsive** nourishment or healing (e.g., in response to some event or in preparation for an event)

- **Habitual**, at every shift of attention, and

- **Continual**, as in being tuned into higher vibrations constantly.

It is the only way I know of to get from occasional bliss and higher consciousness to frequent bliss and higher consciousness, and then to perpetual bliss and higher consciousness.

How about you? How often do you take in spiritual nourishment? Are you getting enough?

FIFTY-SEVEN

There Are a Lot
of Amazingly Talented People!

Quite embarrassingly, I used to live in a world where there was only one right answer, and I usually got it first. I was so wrapped up in my own ego and brilliance, that I simply couldn't see the brilliance of others.

And I was surprised to learn that there were other bright people, too! As I expanded my circle of relationships, I even came to meet people who were smarter than I was.

Then I began to see the talents that they had that I didn't have at all. They could dance and do athletic things that I couldn't even begin to do. They could draw and create art in ways that seemed magical to me.

Then I came to understand emotional intelligence, and realized there were people who were more self-aware, people who could manage their emotions better, understand other people better, and who were quite gifted at forming and managing relationships. I couldn't do any of those things.

And lately, I have come to be amazed at how brilliant and talented other people can be even more. I now see that great ideas can come from anyone, and that includes children and even toddlers.

How about you? Do you see and appreciate the genius in others? Do you see and appreciate your own genius?

FIFTY-EIGHT

The Law of Empowerment

I was surprised to learn about the Law of Empowerment, how that when we become empowered in one area of our lives, it serves to make us feel more powerful in other areas of our lives. When we practice being powerful in one way, it serves to help us be powerful in all ways. It serves to build our self-image of being a powerful person and decreases our fear.

Likewise, when we allow ourselves to be weak in one area of our lives, it serves to disempower us in other areas of our lives. It serves to build on our self-image of being a weak person and increases our fear. That is one of the key reasons that discipline is essential to growth – a lack of discipline teaches us that we are weak at a subconscious level. Being disciplined helps give us a sense of control and empowerment.

And it is one of the main reasons that people break rules, and laws, and commitments: because cheating and getting away with something makes them feel more powerful. People rebel in order to feel more powerful. People sabotage those in power in order to feel more powerful by getting back at them in some way.

And it is the reason we like to play games. Winning a game, or at least playing well, also serves to empower us and helps make us feel clever, competent, talented, powerful, and safe. Those who watch us play often live vicariously through us, and they feel more empowered through that association. Likewise, we both feel disempowered when we lose or play poorly, or more likely, we will tell ourselves that "it was just a game".

How about you? Do you feel empowered when you win a game? When you feel powerful in one area of life, do you feel empowered in other areas, too?

FIFTY-NINE
Separate Languages

I was eager to change my major in college to Philosophy at the start of my sophomore year. A few short weeks later, I was even more excited to change it to something else.

I was surprised to learn that almost every philosophical argument wasn't an argument over logic, but rather a disagreement over assumptions and definitions. Those who were arguing or discussing a particular point of view couldn't agree on the facts and the definitions of many of the terms that they were using.

Now, I think that 90% of all disagreements are caused by differences in terminology. But it takes a pretty alert and aware person to realize it.

And anyone who ever says "that's not what the word means" just doesn't get that we speak different languages. The much, much wiser expression is "that's not what the word means to me" or even "I don't think that's the meaning many or most people ascribe to that word", or "I invite you to consider another definition for that word".

Here's a little example: a few days ago, I was getting dinner ready for the family. When the food was warmed up, I told my wife it was "ready". When she got into the kitchen, she was disappointed to find out that the table wasn't set and the food was still on the stove. She said it wasn't "ready". So we each had our own definition of the term. We didn't argue about it, rather, we chuckled over the differences in our language – because my wife, Sherry, is pretty wise herself. ☺

SIXTY
Separate Realities

When I was growing up, I didn't know anyone who had visions or communicated with ethereal beings. There was some talk about some strange old great-aunt who had some mystery about her, but no one I knew claimed to be psychic in any way.

That might have been because the church that I went to when I was a child frowned upon such things. Mother Mary notwithstanding, others who saw visions or had precognitive dreams were victims of the work of the devil. Good Christian people in my town had no such experiences.

So I was really surprised to learn that some people see and talk with Angels. They receive guidance and act on it. They talk with God and God talks back to them! They feel like they can predict the future, effect remote healing, cast out demons, and bring your soul back into alignment.

The best that I can muster these days is an occasional precognitive or predictive lucid dream. These are occurring more and more often as I grow older, and to be truthful, I really want them to.

Others believe in some really strange theories. They think there are secret societies that have $trillions in wealth, control the world, and enslave us all. Others believe that the holocaust never happened, that men never landed on the moon, and the US government brought down the twin towers as an excuse for war.

They are experiencing far different realities than I do.

And while it can be challenging to deal with those who are heavy into those conspiracy theories, I guess I am a little bit jealous of those who tell me how wonderful it is to talk and walk with the angels. ☺

How about you? Does your reality include angels, demons, or other forms of psychic events? What do you think about such things?

SIXTY-ONE

Reincarnation

This is a big one. It doesn't make sense to scientists and engineers (and a LOT of other people), but I was very surprised to become convinced that reincarnation is true, or at least the best explanation for a collection of miraculous phenomena.

What convinced me was the story of James Leininger as recounted in a book about his phenomenal experiences, *Soul Survivor*. Little James started having memories of a previous life as a fighter pilot when he was two and a half years old. It's an amazing story.

Dr. Jim Tucker, a psychiatrist at the University of Virginia, is the author *of Life Before Life: A Scientific Investigation of Children's Memories of Previous Lives*, which recounts over four decades of research into the childhood memories, which simply could not have been influenced by any current life experience. It's just the icing on the cake for me.

And believing in reincarnation opens up a lot of other possibilities, such as the Akashic Records, life contracts, and more.

Reincarnation isn't the end of the story – it's just a doorway to a greater truth.

How about you? Do you believe in reincarnation? Do you know anyone who has had memories of a past life?

SIXTY-TWO

Physical Reality vs. Spiritual Reality

I was very surprised to discover that there seems to be two different sets of laws governing our realities: the physical laws of creation and the spiritual laws of creation.

It was such an impactful discovery that I wrote an entire book about it entitled *The Levels of Creation.* Here's an excerpt from the introduction:

> There are many spiritual systems and sciences that address the issue of how we create things on this Earth, and they are often times in conflict with each other.
>
> The disciplines that teach "The Law of Attraction" and similar concepts focus on how our thoughts and feelings – our Energetic Signature – determines everything that we see, feel and experience.
>
> But scientists and engineers know that in order to build things, there is a completely different set of laws and guidelines that apply.
>
> On the one hand, no one ever created anything that was not first envisioned. And on the other hand, no one ever built a building without working with building materials. Sitting in a chair and envisioning a structure will never get the job done.
>
> When we are functioning at the Spiritual Level of Creation, the Physical Laws are completely unnecessary and may be seen as a total waste of time. So some people choose to ignore the Physical Laws to their detriment. In the worst cases, they spend the majority of their time in meditation and prayer – getting their minds right – and fail to take action at all. They wonder why their visions are not being rapidly manifested and their prayers are not being answered in the way they would like.

When we are operating exclusively at the Physical Level, the Spiritual Laws may seem totally ridiculous and even insane. So engineers and scientists tend to discount them, and focus on creating without them. They fail to develop their full potential and discount the power of visioning and intention.

The Great Paradox is that the Spiritual Laws of Creation often seem to be the opposite of the Physical Laws of Creation. The Spiritual Level is one of Omnipotence and unlimited power and resources. The Physical Level is one of limitations and careful planning.

And it was a great comfort to me to be able to compare, understand, and reconcile these different perspectives.

What a surprise!

How about you? Do you see the different levels now? Does this make sense to you?

SIXTY-THREE

Creation is an "Inside Out" Game

I was very surprised to learn that creation is an "inside out" game. First, you become the person you need to be, then you are able to manifest the outcome you seek.

That doesn't make a lot of sense to most people, and it certainly didn't make any sense to me when I was younger. I was focused on the external, physical world, the doing and the having, as the key to my wellbeing. And I was surprised to run into subconscious blocks that prevented me from getting the success I wanted.

Subconscious blocks are the bane of many people. They hesitate to pick up the phone and call a prospect. They stop short of having a critical conversation with an employee, boss, or family member. They fail to complete an assignment or even start one in the first place. And they don't have enough self-awareness to feel their fear, much less to explore it and deal with it effectively.

They don't see the importance of doing the inner work, because that simply isn't taught in school, or too often, in the home.

I found that the best approach for me is to focus on my mindset, then on my methods, and then finally on my momentum. First, I get my head on straight and believe in myself, then I make a plan, and then I take action.

How about you? Do you focus on your mindset before taking action, or do you just jump into it? Have you ever struggled to do something or achieve something without really knowing why?

SIXTY-FOUR

It's the Pain that Wakes Us Up

People who have experienced tremendous tragedies and hardships in their lives (e.g., Ron Heagy and Victor Frankel) have discovered that they could tune into peace and joy and love regardless of their circumstance.

That was quite surprising to me. I think it is normal to believe that people who have lost limbs, been paralyzed, or who have been tortured in some way would just give up. And while I am sure that some do, many are able to refocus, let go of the pain and the loss, and connect to a new source of comfort and inspiration.

They embrace a new self-image and they develop a deep inner strength. The pain wakes them up.

On a smaller scale, it is the hardships and challenges that we all go through that help us discover our limiting beliefs and habits of thought and action that just don't serve us anymore.

We face the challenges and the pain, we go through the "refiner's fire", and come out the other side a stronger, more compassionate, and loving person.

Believe me, I wish it were not so, and I denied it for a long time. But it's true: it's the pain that wakes us up.

> *How about you? Have you had challenges in your life that facilitated your personal and spiritual growth?*

SIXTY-FIVE
Modern Day Masters

I was surprised to learn that there really are Masters and Gurus in this world who can do some miraculous things. They have Jesus-level skills. I'm not one of them. 😊

When I was young, I was taught that Jesus would come again, but always expected his name to be "Jesus". Now, I'm not so sure. I think the spirit of Jesus has come many times over the millennia, in a lot of different bodies.

Let me tell you a little about two of them:

Muhammad Subuh Sumohadiwidjojo, aka **Bapak**, was the founder of the Subud movement, a spiritual community. He lived from 1901 to 1987.

Had some intense spiritual experiences in 1932, and thereafter travelled the world establishing and visiting groups of followers. He designed a spiritual exercise called the Latihan Kejiwan (Indonesian for Spiritual Exercise) that facilitates a connection to the divine.

He could do some really amazing things, like simply come up with the answer to complex physics problems, know things about strangers, visit people in their dreams, and effect miraculous healings.

Another master is **Sri Sri Ravishankar**, the founder of The Art of Living Global Organization, was born in 1956 and is still with us today. He began spiritual practice very early in life, and gradually came into his Enlightenment. He designed a breathing exercise, Sudarshan Kriya, as a way to teach people how to relieve stress and experience more happiness in their life.

He has travelled extensively, considers everyone in the world a part of his family, and has done an extensive amount of humanitarian work. He has perhaps 160 million followers. 2.5 million people gathered to celebrate the 25th anniversary of his organization, The Art of Living.

And I think he is the closest thing to Jesus or Buddha walking the earth today.

These are just a couple of examples of Modern Day Jesuses and Buddhas, showing us the possibilities of the human experience.

And consider this: Buddha wasn't a Buddhist, Jesus wasn't a Christian, and Muhammad wasn't a Muslim. It seems the most powerful masters are always doing their own thing. You probably won't find them in your church, temple, or synagogue – you will most likely find them in sacred buildings that their followers have built just for them.

How about you? Do you believe that there have been multiple masters through the ages? Do you believe that someone with Jesus-like gifts could be walking the earth today?

SIXTY-SIX
Lifelong Learning

When I first started my inner work in earnest when I was about 19 years old, I figured it would take me about nine years. I was pretty sure that I would be fully enlightened, whatever that was, by the time I was 28.

Boy was I wrong about that one! The time that it has taken me to even be partially enlightened has been a huge surprise.

I thought the road to enlightenment would be like getting a college degree. You work at it four years, you take a test, and then you get the certificate.

Now, over 50 years later, the lessons keep coming. It seems like I learn something valuable and new practically every day, or at least a few times a week.

I was probably surprised because no adult ever sat down with me and said, "I'm still on my journey". They wanted to be seen as adults instead of as people who were still learning and growing. The concept of "lifelong learning" was introduced after I got out of high school; and before that, I guess people just graduated from high school or college and just shut the learning engine down.

It's an old analogy but a useful one: gaining wisdom is like peeling an onion, except in this case, there are an infinite number of layers. And you don't have to cry all the time. ☺

How about you? Did anyone sit you down and talk about how gaining wisdom is a lifelong process?

SIXTY-SEVEN

Lessons are Learned in Different Sequences

The journey to enlightenment isn't like a course where you take lesson one, then lesson two, and so on, in a predictable and regimented manner. Surprise! Everyone learns at their own pace and in their own sequence.

A message that doesn't mean anything to me may be the perfect message for someone else. A teacher who isn't for me in the moment might be the perfect teacher for someone else.

We learn when we are ready. I wonder if all of the lessons are available to us all of the time (especially now in the age of the Internet) and we just learn the one that we are ready to learn in the moment.

And here's an amazing thing about that: it means that practically anyone may know something that I don't know, or that they can at least remind me of a lesson that I have forgotten.

And it means that practically anyone and anything can be my teacher, and that includes children, birds, dogs, cats, and bugs.

It means that EVERYONE is here to teach me a lesson; they are all here to help me gain wisdom, either by showing me what to do or what not to do.

When the student is ready, the teacher appears.

How about you? Have you been surprised when someone younger or less fortunate than you had some wisdom to share?

SIXTY-EIGHT

Some People Prefer
an Imperfect Teacher

I was really surprised to find out that some people prefer an imperfect teacher. I was surprised that I didn't have to wait until I was as powerful and wise as Jesus and Sri Sri to be the perfect guide to someone else.

For years, I waited to really get out there and share the wisdom I have gained because I was still on my journey. I didn't want to be a hypocrite. More than anyone else, I was aware of, and was dealing with, my imperfections.

But then a friend told me that he didn't want to have a perfect teacher. He thought that being with a truly advanced soul, or someone that we perceive to be far above us, can be intimidating. It can trigger enormous amounts of self-doubt and fear.

People can lose hope when the road seems too long. But when the guide is REAL and perhaps just a few paces ahead of us, we are encouraged that, despite our own imperfections, we can make it to where they are.

When the teacher is vulnerable and humble, it is easier for the student to be humble, open, and vulnerable, too.

Knowing that helps me reach out and share all of these surprises with you.

How about you? Do you demand that your teachers are perfect? Are they pretending to be, and fooling you with their act?

SIXTY-NINE
How Many Paths There Are

When I was young, I was taught that there was only "one way" to heaven, and it was through the beliefs and practices of my church. I think that there was some appreciation and consideration given to churches that were similar to us, but my Catholic friend across the street? He was doomed. And Jewish kids? Well, they were going to hell, too. There was nothing I could do to save them, except of course, to try to convert them to my faith.

So I was surprised to learn that there were other paths to Spirit, to Enlightenment, to Heaven, and that some of them were vastly superior to the one I was taught so early on.

Now I see that there are many Spiritual traditions "with a heart". I have beautiful, wonderful, saintly friends who are Protestant, Catholic, Jewish, Hindu, Native American, and Muslim.

Each of them has found their way out of the darkness and into the light by walking a different path.

And I am reminded of the old Hindu saying: "There are many paths up the mountain. Only a fool runs around the bottom telling everyone else they are on the wrong path."

One of the most important things about choosing and walking a path is that we don't need to learn all of them, because we can't follow all of them at the same time anyway. We only need to walk one at a time.

So if you are stalled or stuck, then think about changing your path. Otherwise, walk it.

> *How about you? Are walking a path with a heart? Are you looking for a new one? Were you told that there was only one?*

SEVENTY

There are Thousands of Ways to Shift Your Energy

I was surprised to learn that not only are there many spiritual traditions that can lead to enlightenment, there are also thousands of ways to shift energy and raise your vibration. There are a thousand things you can do right now to take a step towards enlightenment.

You can take a deep breath, stretch, or take a walk. You can slow down your thoughts or simply think different thoughts. You can have a drink or grab a bite to eat. You can say a poem or listen to some music.

The list goes on and on.

I think I have learned a few hundred ways to shift my energy. I have a long list of songs, poems, insights, and practices that I can choose from whenever I sense that it is time to raise my vibration.

My ways are not likely to be the same as your ways. I like different music. I like to exercise and stretch my body in ways that might be uncomfortable and counterproductive to you. My ways are my ways. Your ways are your ways.

So what would you like to do now? How are you choosing to shift RIGHT NOW?

How about you? Do you have a list of things you can do right now to shift your energy and raise your vibration? Are you doing them regularly?

SEVENTY-ONE
Transcending the Path

I was surprised to learn that eventually, when you get close to the destination, you have to let go of the path.

You have to transcend the mindset of "I am becoming" and come to the place of "I am".

You have to let go of the words, the labels, the rituals, and the traditions. They serve you for a while, but the closer you come to Enlightenment, the less they matter, and the more they hold you back.

You have to stop thinking of yourself as Christian, Buddhist, Jewish, Muslim, LDS, etc. You have to think of yourself as Spirit, and then become Spirit. Many religious people hate this idea, of course, because they are so attached to their path. They find comfort and safety in their path, and they are in some way, large or small, afraid of leaving it behind.

They get so focused on the path that they forget about the destination. They haven't learned how to just Let Go and return to the Loving Awareness and the Silent Emptiness of the Eternal Now.

But you are not like them. You can learn to Just Be.

I Am.

Are you?

How about you? Are you ready to transcend your path? Are you ready to Return to Spirit?

SEVENTY-TWO
The Power of Words

I was surprised to learn that words can be so powerful. I was even more surprised to learn that "words are labels on concepts" and "words have energy".

What that means is that every word that we hear, speak, or say silently to ourselves has an energetic power to it. Words can lift us to the heavens or keep us trapped in the pit of darkness.

Some years ago, I noticed that certain words – just the words alone – shifted my energy. For example, when I said "jubilation!" or "eager!", my spirits were lifted. That's because the words triggered a memory and subconscious response toward joy and empowerment.

So I made a list of 2500+ of my favorite words. And more recently, I made a list of over 300 words that are among the most powerful of them.

I found that words and the energies they represent can be very effective tools of Awakening. They can be used alone or together to form very effective mantras.

Sometimes I use them in combinations where they become balancing energies, for example:

- Connected, Protected, Guided, and Loved

- Awakened, Lighthearted, and Kind

- Peaceful, Joyful, Powerful, Wise, and Loving

- Mindful, Mellow, and Lighthearted

- Awakened, Aware, and Cheerful

- Grateful, Humble, and Amazed

- Confident, Playful, Powerful, and Free

- Humble, Light-hearted, Compassionate, Courageous, and Surrendered
- Aligned, Focused, and Determined
- Transcendent, Watching, and Loving
- … and so on.

Sometimes the sequence matters a lot, and the words take me on a journey of transformation such as:

- I See, I Believe, I Choose, I Transform, I Become, I Am.
- I See, I Feel, I Love, I Heal
- I Detach, I Shift, I Am
- I Awaken, I Remember, I Relax, I Smile, I Love, I See, I Am
- I Awaken, I Embrace the Silence, and I Am
- … and so on.

I have dozens, even hundreds, of these combinations and sequences. Sometimes a single word will do, other times I find great value in a large combination of words, or a sequence of thought and action that is dozens of steps long. It depends on how far away I am from Spirit – the further away I am, the more words I need in order to complete the journey.

All I have to do is to remember to use them.

And I encourage you to remember this: words can heal, and words can harm. Be careful of your self-talk and be careful of what you say to others.

How about you? Are there some words that you like and others that trigger you in some way?

SEVENTY-THREE

The New Spiritual Teachers are as Good as the Old Ones

I was taught early on that the Bible was the only true word of God, and that every other message was inferior. Others see the Koran or some other religious text as sacrosanct, infallible, and "the best."

So I was surprised to learn that it simply wasn't true for me. There are lots of great teachers and books on their teachings. Divine inspiration didn't stop 2,000 years ago. To think that it did is to sell us short and place unnecessary limitations on the Divine.

And I think there is probably a good case to be made that newer teachings, such as those from Eckhart Tolle, Byron Katie, Sri Sri Ravishankar, etc. are actually more effective in some ways. Well, at least they are for me.

Modern spiritual teachers use modern language. They use stories and analogies in their messages that are current and with which I can really resonate.

And as far as I can tell, the modern teachers are as Enlightened and connected as anyone has ever been.

So I listen to them all: the ancient ones, the new ones, and the ones that come to me every day.

How about you? Who are your favorite spiritual teachers? Do you think they are on the level of Jesus, Buddha, and Muhammad?

SEVENTY-FOUR
The Power of Believing

This is one of the biggest surprises of all: the act of believing is more important than what is believed. If you believe in yourself, divinity, and transformation, nothing else matters.

It was never the path that mattered. The path just needs to allow and facilitate the believing. It's the believing that creates the reality. The path just gives you a framework that allows you to believe.

That's why numerology, snake charming, tarot cards, and all of the religions and spiritual systems work to a point.

When we share a path with others, the most important thing is our belief in the path, and that's what inspires others to begin believing for themselves.

This is tough to imagine. We often think the power is in the external world rather than in ourselves, and that others have the power to teach us or save us. We think that the power to transform ourselves is in the other people or in the path.

But to me, it's just not true. Each of us holds the key to our own salvation. Each of us has the ability to believe.

It is the confidence level of the belief, the power of the belief, the purity and completeness of the belief that makes the difference.

And Certainty, well that's the greatest power there is.

How about you? Do you believe in the power of believing? Do you believe in the power of Certainty?

SEVENTY-FIVE

The Many Flavors of Enlightenment

I was surprised to learn that enlightened souls, while having many similarities, can be quite different in their expression of Divinity. There are many flavors of enlightenment.

They can be peaceful, joyful, powerful, wise, and reflective, and consumed by Love. I suspect that they are any and all of these things whenever they want, but it is difficult to express all the flavors at the same time because this whole time-and-space thing limits Divine expression.

That's why we see Enlightened people with different personalities. Eckhart Tolle is different from Sri Sri Ravishankar, and both are different from Byron Katie. They are each expressing Divinity in their own way. Their messages are filtered through their culture, language, and their experiences to come out a little different.

And as we make progress on our journeys, we may develop different gifts of the spirit, including the ability to create and manipulate physical reality (such as healing, manifesting, and attracting), ethereal perception and communication (as with intuition, precognition, and psychic communication), and we may develop the ability to simply have presence (to have an extremely high vibration of peace, joy, strength, wisdom, and love.)

Yes, there are many flavors of Enlightenment – far more than the 31 flavors of ice cream at Baskin Robbins.

How about you? What is your favorite or most common expression of Enlightenment? What are your gifts?

SEVENTY-SIX

Divine Love Is a Choice

I was surprised to learn that Unconditional Love, true Divine Love, isn't a response – it is a Choice.

For much of my life, I loved people, things, and experiences that triggered my Love. My Love was a response to those external things. My Love was conditional.

Sometimes it was a girl, sometimes it was a great song, and Oh Boy! – do I love ice cream!

But as my Love grew and I experienced more and more depth and completeness to my Loving, I came to see that Divine Love was a State of Being. It wasn't a response to something external at all – it was a Choice of mindset and energy, a Choice of a way of life.

And I learned how hard it was for me to make that Choice when encountering things that usually frighten me or make me angry. Certain people, especially some politicians I won't name, people who are abusive and rude and combative, I found very difficult to Love.

But now, more often than not, I make that Choice. I enter into Divine Love, and it becomes my State of Being.

And like the sun, it Shines on Everyone equally. It is independent, pure, complete, and limitless.

It is Divine.

How about you? Is your Love a triggered response, or is it a choice? Does your Love (sometimes) shine on everyone?

SEVENTY-SEVEN
How Truly Amazing Life Is

I am surprised and amazed to wake up every day just being surprised and amazed at this incredible human experience.

I'm amazed that I have hands and fingers and feet and toes.

I'm amazed that I am able to see and think and feel.

I'm amazed that I have running water and cars and computers.

I'm amazed so often that I live in a near constant state of amazement and wonder and awe.

Sometimes I feel like I have just awoken from a 2,000-year-old dream, and just yesterday I was sleeping on dirt, covered up by animal skins, foraging for food and looking for water. And then suddenly I am standing in my kitchen and going to the refrigerator to get a little snack. Whoa!

And I wonder sometimes if this is my imagination or a past life memory.

What I do know is that the difference is Amazing.

I wrote this little poem years ago that expresses my amazement, entitled *How Can It Be?*

There once was a man from down yonder

Who looked up at the sky with great wonder

Thinking "How can it be

That creatures like me

Exist to look upwards and ponder?"

This same common man among men

Oft chuckled, whilst stroking his chin.

Thinking "How can it be

That creatures like me

Have such latent power within?"

How can it be that I am alive? How can it be that I am sitting here in a castle of rock and wood typing these words? How can it be that I have a physical body and thought and consciousness? How can it be that I live in a physical world, yet I can create reality from my thoughts? How can it be that some people see the future and get messages in non-physical ways? How can it be that life exists in so many forms?

How can it be that I have an occasional lucid dream that comes true?

How can it be?

How about you? Do you take this human experience for granted, or are you amazed, too?

SEVENTY-EIGHT
Love Them All

I was walking through a large store a few months ago and I was surprised to suddenly feel like everyone there was a precious child – MY precious child – and I began to love them unconditionally.

I was surprised at how much I loved people who were so different than me. They had different colored skin, they wore different clothes, and they spoke different languages – and it made no difference.

I was surprised at how wonderful it feels to be consumed by love and to be connected to all of them.

I was amazed to look at someone and suddenly see and imagine all of the moments of their lifetime. I saw them as an infant, a toddler, a young boy or girl, a young adult, a mature adult, and as an old man or woman. I saw them on their death bed. I saw all of their moods: the joy, the sadness, the anger, and the love. I saw the totality of their human experience.

I saw that they were all but spiritual children, doing the best they could to empower themselves and feel safe.

And I loved everyone and everything that I saw.

And of course, I wrote a poem about it, and then made it into a song:

Love them All, Love them All, Love them All
The young and the old
The timid, the bold
The rich and the poor
The charmer, the bore
The silly, the serious
The known, the mysterious

The tiny, the tall
Love them All, Love them All, Love them All.

The dark and the light
The dull and the bright
The shallow, the deep
The awake, the asleep
The happy, the sad
The calm and the mad,
.The friend and the foe
The ex and the beau
The large and the small
Love them All, Love them All, Love them All.
Love them All, Love them All, Love them All.

So how about you? Who do you love? Who do you not love? Do you practice loving everyone you meet - and everyone you have yet to meet?

SEVENTY-NINE
Life is But a Dream

And this is one of the most surprising things of all: the little children's song, "Row, Row, Row Your Boat" – it was right: life is but a dream. We each experience our own reality.

And of course, I wrote a little poem about this many years ago that captures the surprise for me:

The Search

I've hunted and searched for 50-plus years

From the mountains to the sea.

I've read many masters, meditated, and prayed

With the utmost sincerity.

But despite my deep longing to find some grand meaning

In life, it appears to me,

That life is but a persistent, lucid dream.

What else could it be?

And who the heck is the dreamer, and who the heck is me?

And whenever I awaken, whatever shall I see?

And in the next reality, whoever shall I be?

Life is but a dream. And almost no one knows it.

But now, you do.

How about you? Are you surprised to learn that life is but a dream, too?

EIGHTY
Enlightenment is Easy

And perhaps my final surprise is the best one of all... I woke up one morning to find that Enlightenment is Easy...

It is Easy to be Awakened.

It is Easy to be Cheerful.

It is Easy to be Strong.

It is Easy to be Wise.

It is Easy to Surrender.

And it's Easy to Love.

And my wish for you is that you will

Practice being at your Best,

Practice Awakening,

Day after Day,

Moment by Moment,

Until Enlightenment becomes Easy for you, too.

How about you? Is Enlightenment Easy for you, too? If not, Keep Practicing... it Will Be.

About the Author

Paul Hoyt has been on the road to Enlightenment for well over 50 years, and is the creator of Mind Sequencing, a revolutionary approach to personal development and stress relief.

He loves to have meaningful conversations about the nature of reality and the development of consciousness. He studies the masters and does inner work for hours every day. He loves thinking and talking about the meaning of life and human potential. He loves transformational tools that work.

This is his sixth inspirational work. He published *Remember - A Simple and Gentle Pathway to Spirit* in 2005, and *The Practice of Awakening – 150 Ways to Raise Your Consciousness Whenever You Choose* in 2010. He is the best-selling author of *The Practice of Awakening II – The First Light of Joy* (2013), and the privately published works *The Levels of Creation* (2016) and *Curing Racism* (2016-2019).

You can learn more about him and his teachings at www.MindSequencing.com and www.PaulHoyt.com.

And, oh yes, he continues to be surprised every day. ☺

www.ingramcontent.com/pod-product-compliance
Lightning Source LLC
Chambersburg PA
CBHW051722090426
42738CB00010B/2041